A Piano Chord Book You Can Actually Use!

By Aaron Whitehead

© March 2008

Table of Contents

Introduction

This book is designed with the beginning piano student in mind. It is made to assist in learning how the piano, and music in general, works. In order to make this as thorough as possible, the following page of general and piano specific information has been included.

The piano is made up of keys. Each key represents a different pitch. In music, the name given to an individual pitch, or key on the piano, comes from the first 7 letters of the alphabet: A, B, C, D, E, F, and G. The keys then continue to repeat. So, after G would come A again. Figure 1 below shows each key on the piano and its designated name. The key with the red dot identifies middle C, so called because it is the C closest to the center of the piano keyboard.

Figure 1

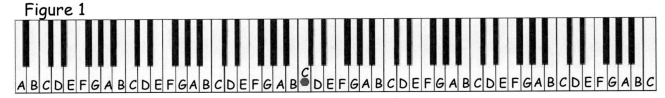

The distance between two notes on the piano with the same letter name is called an octave. The piano keyboard has a total of 7 complete octaves, with a few notes left over. The black notes on the keyboard represent sharps (#) and flats (b). A sharp is a pitch a half-step* above another pitch. So, the black key above (to the right of) middle C is called C#. A flat is a pitch a half-step below another pitch. So, the black key below (to the left of) A is called Ab. All black keys have two names. The black key between middle C and the D above is called C# and Db. Figure 2 demonstrates what a half-step, whole step and octave look like on the piano.

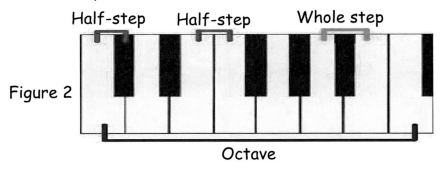

Figure 2

Half-step   Half-step   Whole step

Octave

*Each key on the piano represents a half-step. Two half-steps equal a whole step. So, the distance between the key A and B is a whole step, while the distance between B and C is a half-step.

On the following pages you will see notes represented in different ways. At times the notes will be placed on the piano keyboard so that they are easily identifiable to someone unfamiliar with reading music. They will also be shown on what is called a treble clef. The word clef is used to describe the lines on which written music is notated.

A standard clef will have five lines. Figure 3 shows what the treble clef looks like. The purpose of any clef is to differentiate between notes. The lines and

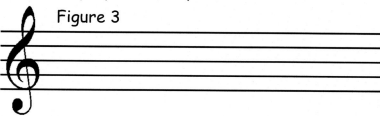

Figure 3

spaces between the lines all represent different notes. One way to help you understand what each of the lines and spaces represent on the treble clef is to think of it by its other name, which is the G clef.

The treble clef figure evolved from the writing of the letter G. So, another way that we could see the treble clef would be something like this:

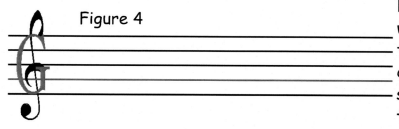

Figure 4

Figure 4 is the treble clef with a common G placed over the clef. The line which the G circles around and creates something like crosshairs is the G line, in this case it is colored red. So, any notes which fall on that line are the G note above middle C.

Figure 5 shows what each line and space of the treble clef represent. These

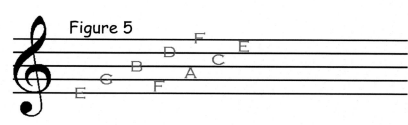

Figure 5

notes are all the notes directly above middle C. There are many ways of going about memorizing what the lines and spaces represent. One obvious one is the spaces spell FACE. For the lines a common saying is "Every Good Boy Does Fine". The first letter of each word represents the note that would fall on that line. Knowing this information is not essential to using this book, however, a basic understanding of how music is notated can aide in learning the material presented on the following pages.

How Chords are Created

A chord is more than one note sounded at the same time. Chords are built by stacking notes on top of each other from within a particular scale. So, the C chord comes from notes within the C scale. The D chord comes from notes within the D scale and so on. Because of the nature of music, chords also appear in more than just one scale. A C scale, for example, also has the G and the F chords in it. Look at Figure 1. This is the C scale. The notes which occur in the C scale are C, D, E, F, G, A, B, and C respectively. By playing a combination of these notes at the same time, we achieve chords.

Figure 1
C Major Scale

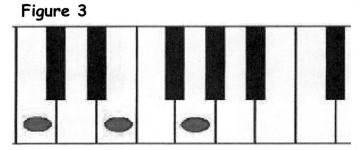

The C chord is made up of the notes C, E, and G. So, by playing these three notes at the same time, we create the C chord. Figure 2 demonstrates which notes are being played from the C scale to form the C chord. Figure 3 shows where these notes fall on the piano keyboard, respectively.

Figure 2
Notes that form a C Major chord

Figure 3

By using the notes from within the C scale we can create a number of different chords. The simplest chords that are created from the notes of the C scale are C Major (C), d minor (Dm), e minor (Em), F Major (F), G Major (G), a minor (Am), and b diminished (Bdim). The pages of this book will demonstrate how chords are created using the notes of the each of the twelve scales.

Some of the chords on the following pages are inversions. This means that the root, or name, of the chord is not the lowest note. This is done to save space, so that all chords in the scale can be played within one octave. Playing inversions of chords also saves the performer time in that it allows him or her to play the notes of the chord as they fall closest to the preceding chord. Playing the three notes that form each chord in any order always produces the same chord.

A chord inversion is made when the arrangement of notes being played on the keyboard are reorganized so that a different note is at the top and bottom of the chord. For example, if the C Major chord is played in root position, that is, the note C is at the bottom, the notes occur as C-E-G from bottom to top. If the performer plays the C which occurs above the G on the piano, the new arrangement is E-G-C from bottom to top. See figure 4. This changes the chord from a root position chord to a first inversion chord. This is done so that the performer can move easily between chords. Most often, playing an inversion of a chord is quicker and easier than playing only root position chords.

Figure 4
Moving the C from the bottom of the chord to the top changes the chord from root position to first inversion.

Root position   First inversion

Three note chords have two inversions: first and second. A first inversion has the note which forms the name of the chord on top. For example, a C chord would be E-G-C from bottom to top, as discussed above. A second inversion has the note which forms the name of the chord second from the top. A C chord in second inversion would be spelled from bottom to top as G-C-E. In order to become more familiar with inversions, an exercise that would be helpful to practice would be to play a chord in root position and work up or down the keyboard making inversions of that chord, naming the inversions and roots as they occur. For example, starting on the C chord which occurs at the middle of the piano keyboard and then progressing to a C first inversion (E-G-C from bottom to top) and then to a C second inversion (G-C-E). The next chord to be played would be a C root position again, but it would be one octave higher than the first C root position chord that was played. Moving in this way, up and down the piano keyboard, will familiarize the player with the position of roots and inversions.

The Chords of the C scale

C Major (root position)

C
I

d minor (root position)

Dm
ii

e minor (root position)

Em
iii

F Major (root position)

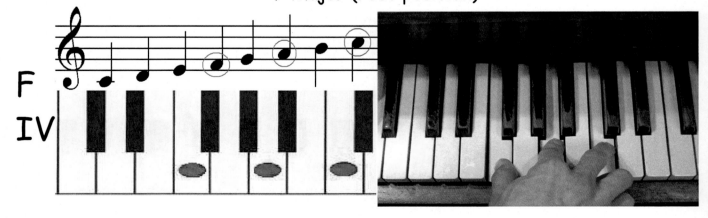

F
IV

G Major (second inversion)

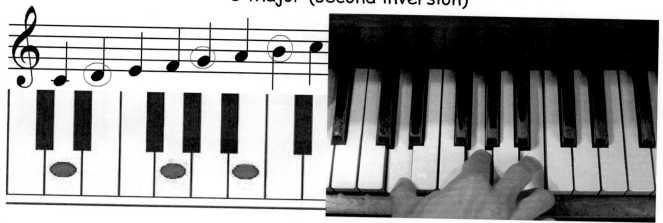

G/D

V

a minor (second inversion)

Am/E

vi

b diminished (first inversion)

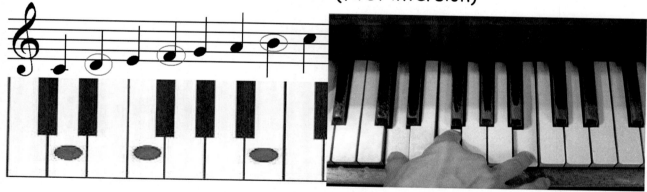

Bdim/D

vii°

C Major (first inversion)

C/E

I

The Chords of the Db/C# scale

Db (C#) Major (root position)

Db
C#
I

Eb (D#) minor (root position)

Ebm
D#m
ii

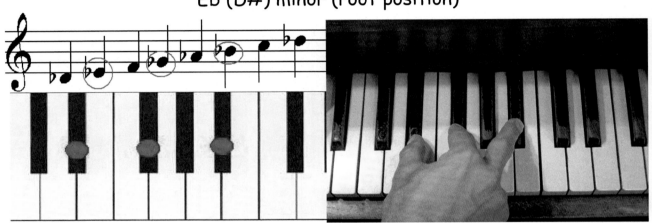

F (E#) minor (root position)

Fm
E#m
iii

Gb (F#) Major (root position)

Gb
F#
IV

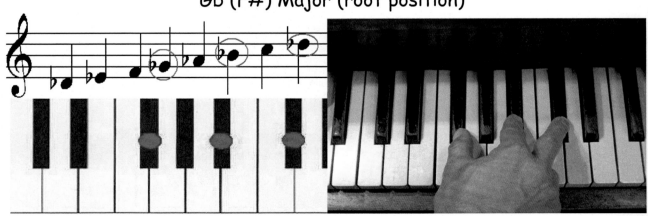

Ab (G#) Major (second inversion)

Ab/Eb
(G#/D#)
V

Bb (a#) minor (second inversion)

Bbm/F
(A#m/E#)
vi

C (b#) diminished (first inversion)

Cdim/Eb
(B#dim/D#)
vii°

Db (C#) Major (first inversion)

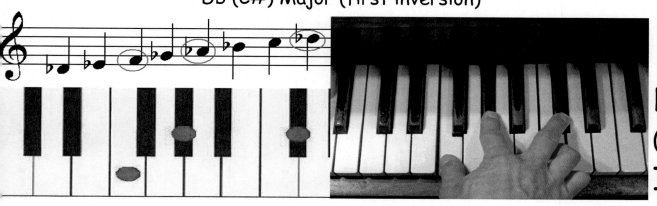

Db/F
(C#/E#)
I

11

The chords of the D Scale

D Major (root position)

D
I

e minor (root position)

Em
ii

f# minor (root position)

F#m
iii

G Major (root position)

G
IV

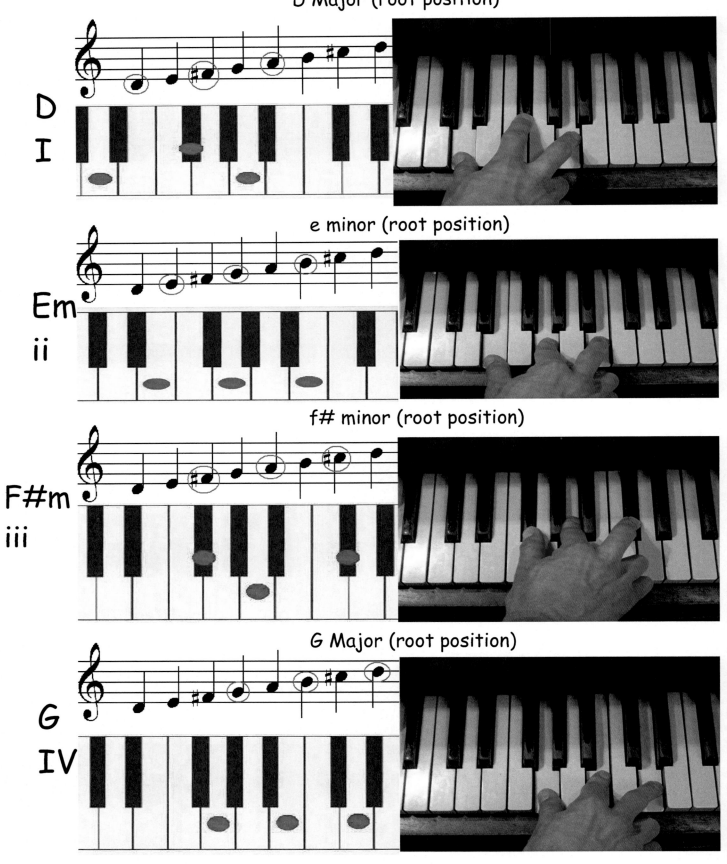

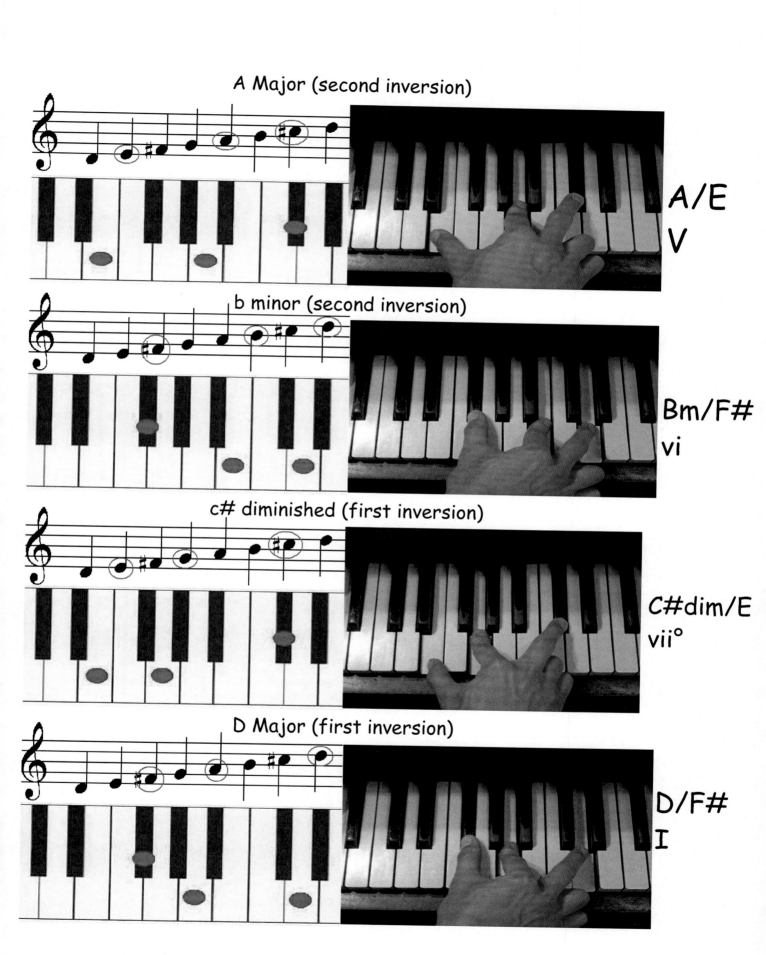

A Major (second inversion)

A/E
V

b minor (second inversion)

Bm/F#
vi

c# diminished (first inversion)

C#dim/E
vii°

D Major (first inversion)

D/F#
I

The Chords of the Eb/D# scale

Eb (D#) Major (root position)

Eb
D#
I

F (E#) minor (root position)

Fm
E#m
ii

G (F*) minor (root position)

Gm
F*m
iii

Ab (G#) Major (root position)

Ab
G#
IV

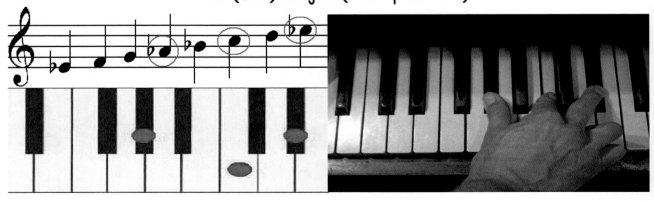

Bb (A#) Major (second inversion)

Bb/F
(A#/E#)
V

C (b#) minor (second inversion)

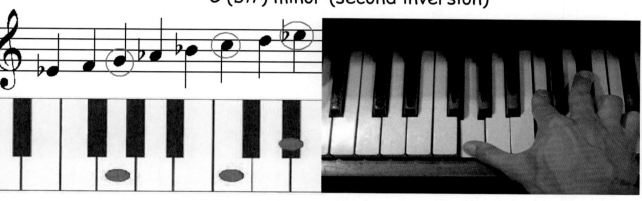

Cm/G
(B#m/F*)
vi

D (C*) diminished (first inversion)

Ddim/F
(C*dim/E#)
vii°

Eb (D#) Major (first inversion)

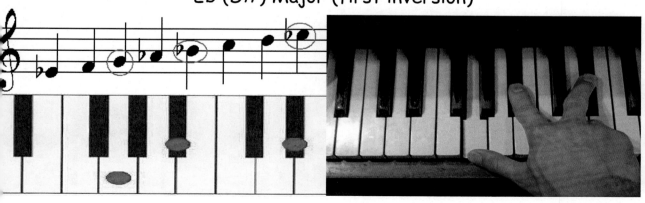

Eb/G
(D#/F*)
I

The chords of the E Scale

E Major (root position)

E
I

f# minor (root position)

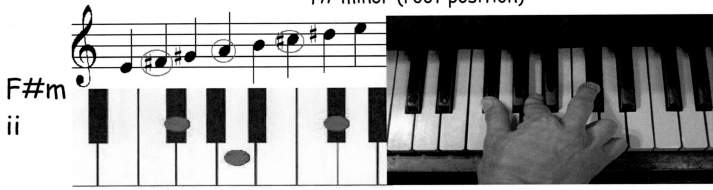

F#m
ii

g# minor (root position)

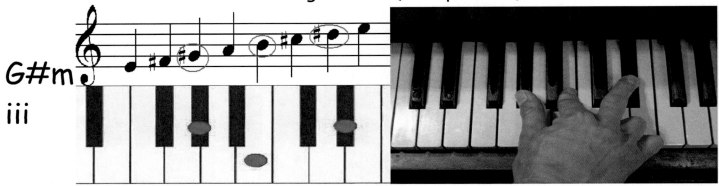

G#m
iii

A Major (root position)

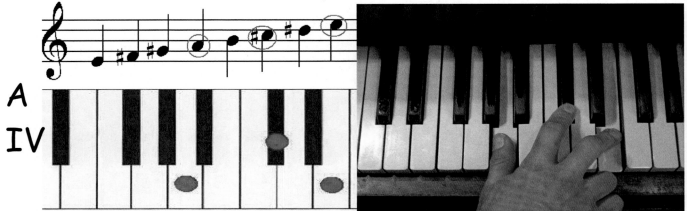

A
IV

B Major (second inversion)

B/F#
V

c# minor (second inversion)

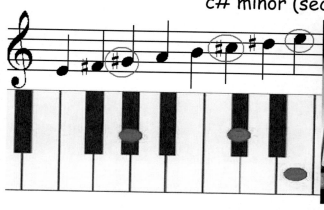

C#m/E
vi

d# diminished (first inversion)

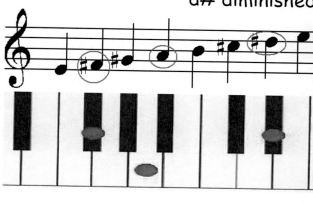

D#dim/F#
vii°

E Major (first inversion)

E/G#
I

The chords of the F Scale

F Major (root position)

F
I

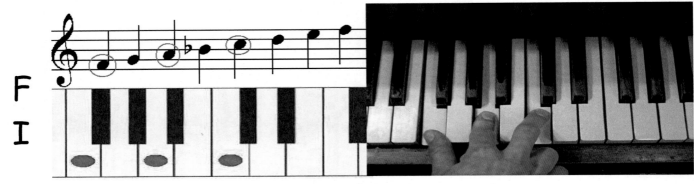

g minor (root position)

Gm
ii

a minor (root position)

Am
iii

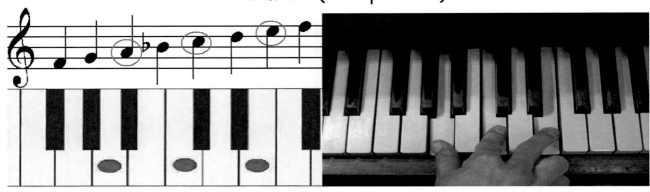

Bb Major (root position)

Bb
IV

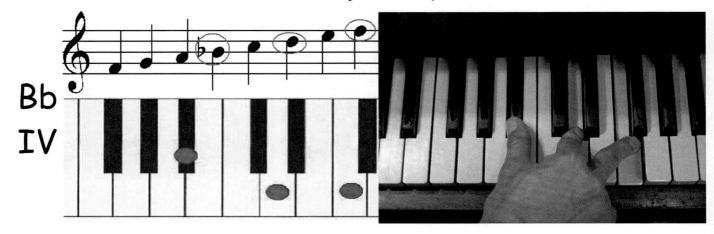

C Major (second inversion)

C/E
V

d minor (second inversion)

Dm/A
vi

e diminished (first inversion)

Edim/G
vii°

F Major (first inversion)

F/A
I

The Chords of the Gb/F# scale

Gb (F#) Major (root position)

Gb
F#
I

Ab (G#) minor (root position)

Abm
G#m
ii

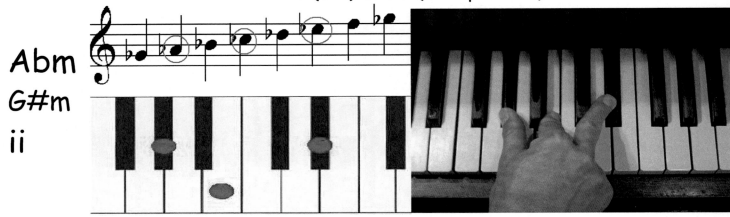

Bb (A#) minor (root position)

Bbm
A#m
iii

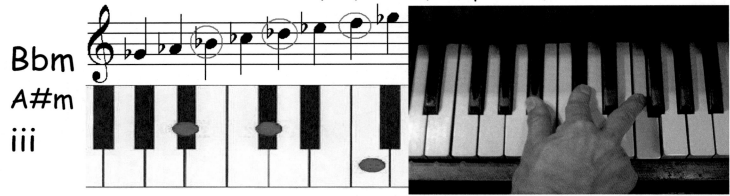

Cb (B) Major (root position)

Cb
B
IV

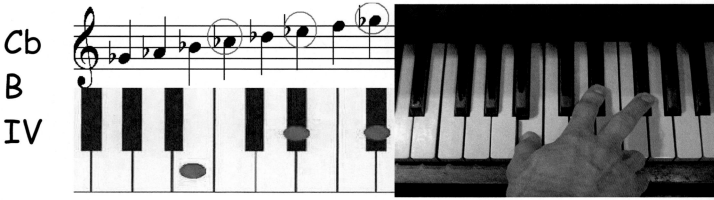

Db (C#) Major (second inversion)

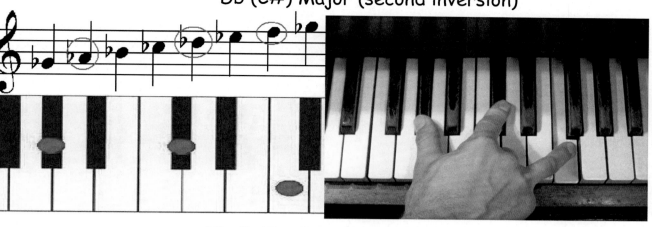

Db/Ab
(C#/G#)
V

Eb (D#) minor (second inversion)

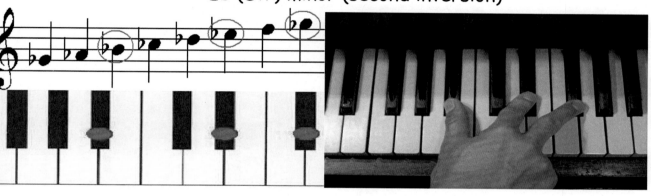

Em/Bb
(D#m/A#)
vi

F (E#) diminished (first inversion)

Fdim/Ab
(E#dim/G#)
vii°

Gb (F#) Major (first inversion)

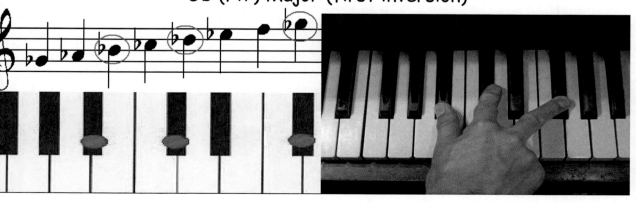

Gb/Bb
(F#/A#)
I

The chords of the G Scale

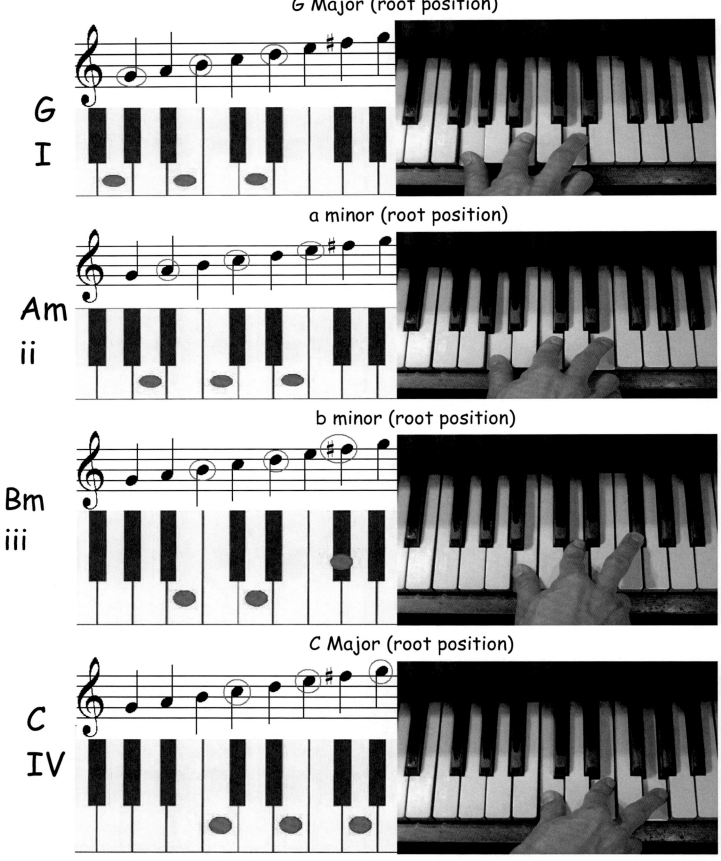

G Major (root position)

G
I

a minor (root position)

Am
ii

b minor (root position)

Bm
iii

C Major (root position)

C
IV

D Major (second inversion)

D/A
V

e minor (second inversion)

Em/B
vi

f# diminished (first inversion)

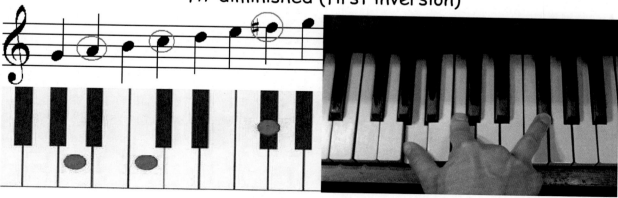

f#dim/A
vii°

G Major (first inversion)

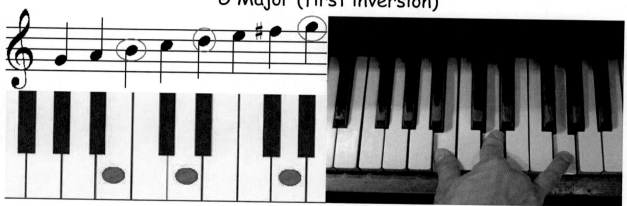

G/B
I

The Chords of the Ab/G# scale

Ab (G#) Major (root position)

Ab
G#
I

Bb (A#) minor (root position)

Bbm
A#m
ii

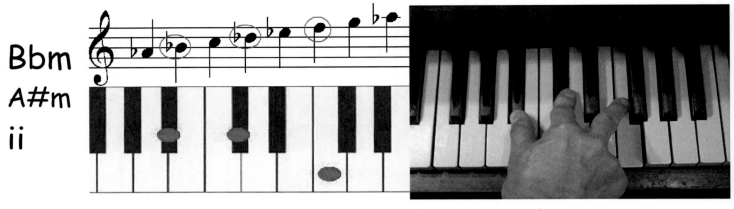

C (B#) minor (root position)

Cm
B#m
iii

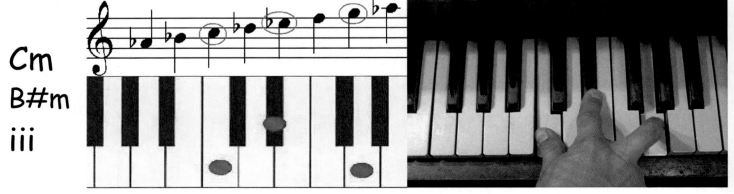

Db (C#) Major (root position)

Db
C#
IV

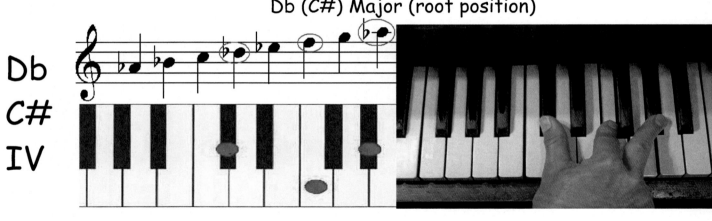

24

Eb (D#) Major (second inversion)

Eb/Bb
(D#/A#)
V

F (E#) minor (second inversion)

Fm/C
(E#m/B#)
vi

G (F*) diminished (first inversion)

Gdim/Bb
(F*dim/A#)
vii°

Ab (G#) Major (first inversion)

Ab/C
(G#/B#)
I

The chords of the A Scale

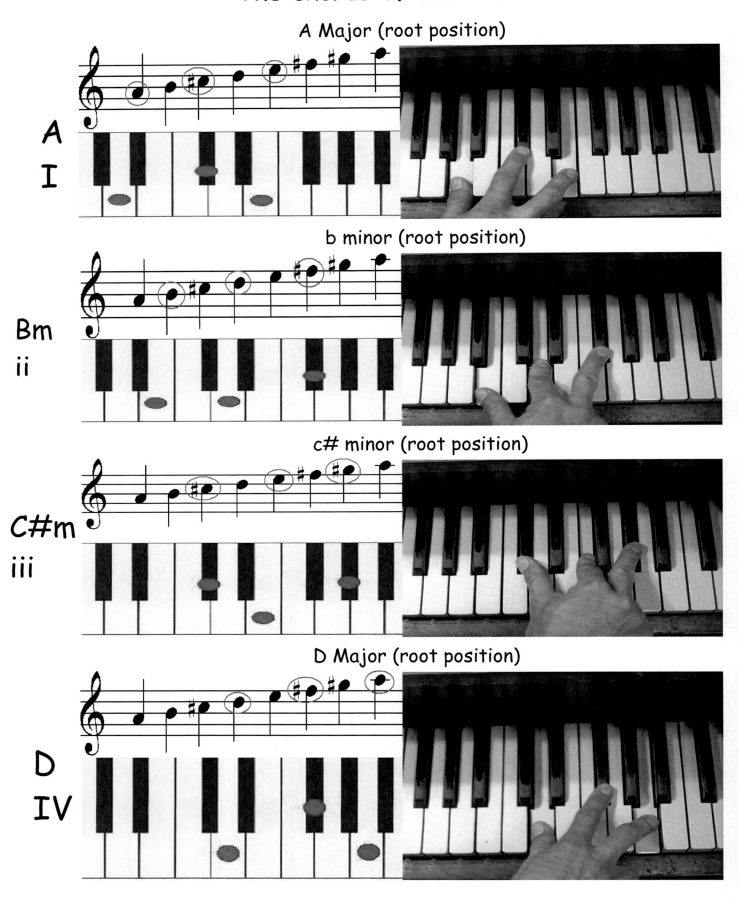

A Major (root position)

A
I

b minor (root position)

Bm
ii

c# minor (root position)

C#m
iii

D Major (root position)

D
IV

E Major (second inversion)

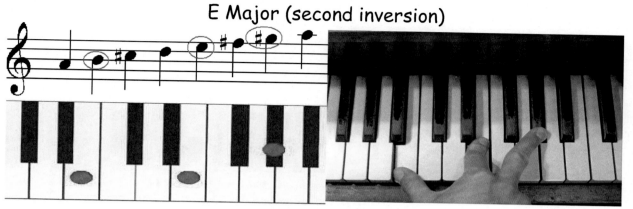

E/B
V

f# minor (second inversion)

F#m/C#
iv

g# diminished (first inversion)

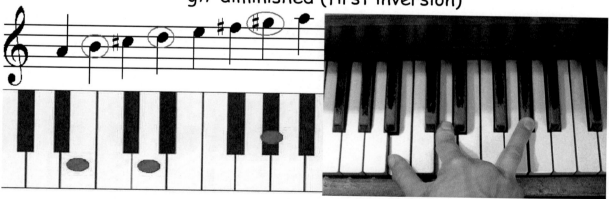

G#dim/B
vii°

A Major (first inversion)

A/C#
I

27

The Chords of the Bb/A# scale

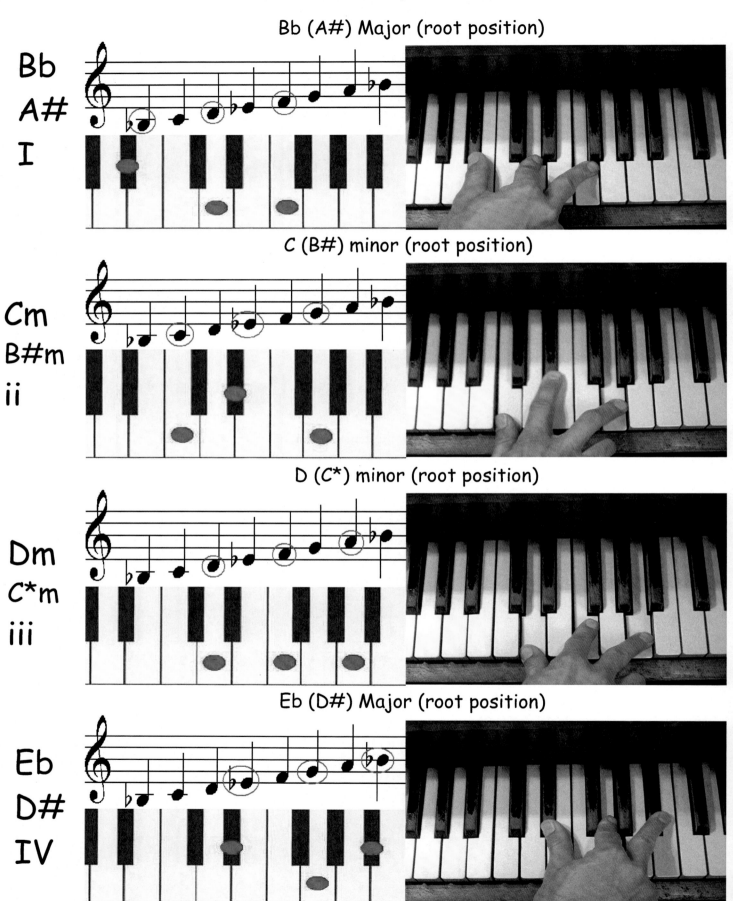

Bb (A#) Major (root position)

Bb
A#
I

C (B#) minor (root position)

Cm
B#m
ii

D (C*) minor (root position)

Dm
C*m
iii

Eb (D#) Major (root position)

Eb
D#
IV

F (E#) Major (second inversion)

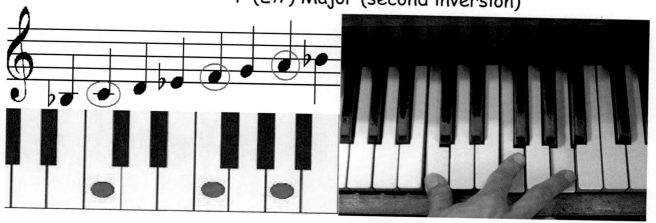

F/C
(E#/B#)
V

G (F*) minor (second inversion)

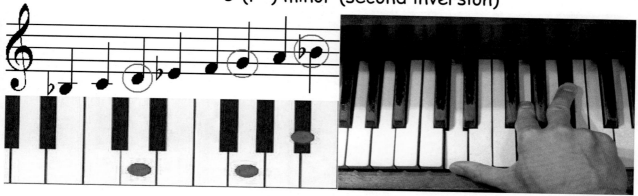

Gm/D
(F*m/C*)
vi

A (G*) diminished (first inversion)

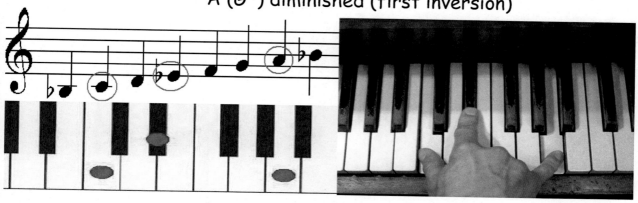

Adim/C
(G*dim/B#)
vii°

Bb (A#) Major (first inversion)

Bb/D
(A#/C*)
I

The chords of the B Scale

B Major (root position)

B
I

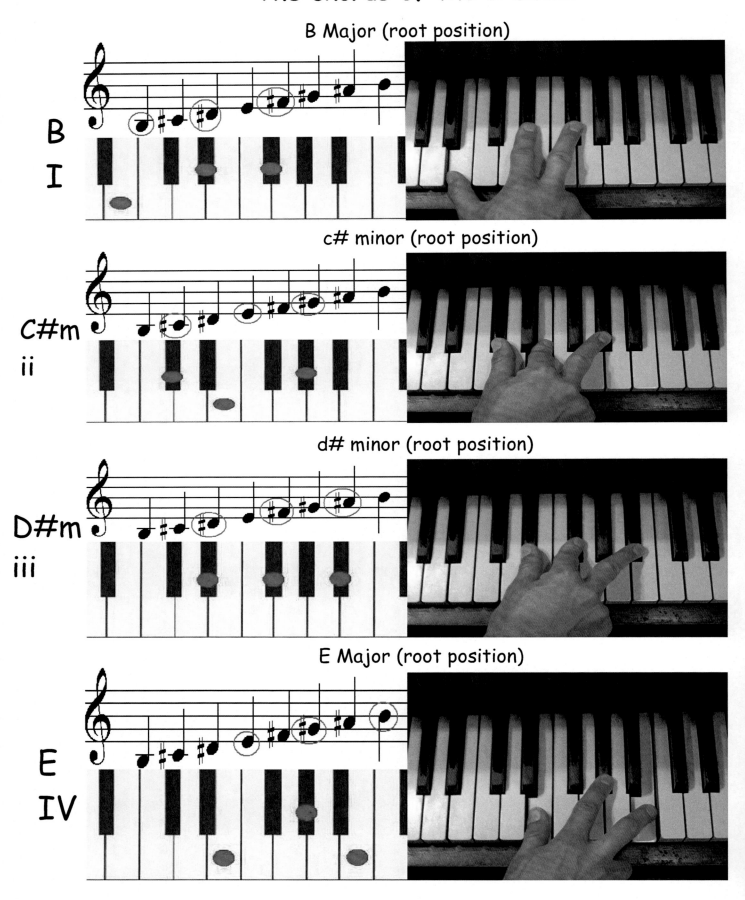

c# minor (root position)

C#m
ii

d# minor (root position)

D#m
iii

E Major (root position)

E
IV

F# Major (second inversion)

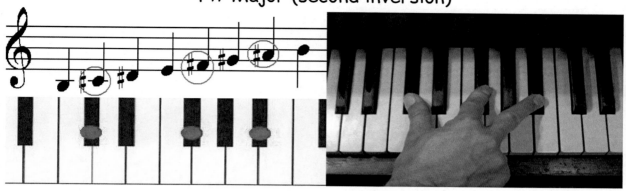

F#/C#

V

g# minor (second inversion)

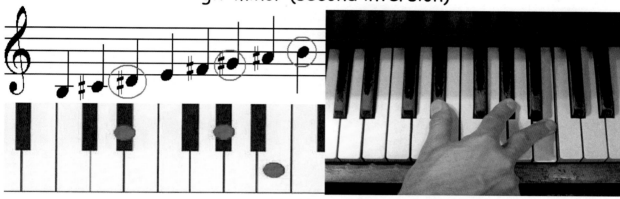

G#m/B

iv

a# diminished (first inversion)

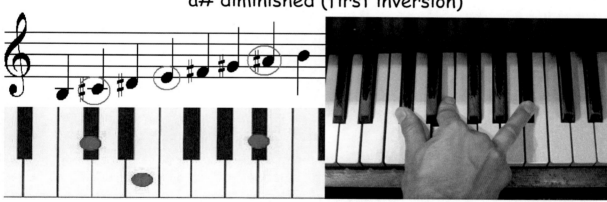

A#dim/C#

vii°

B Major (first inversion)

B/D#

I

A Note on 7ths

Once a player has familiarized themselves with the chords on the previous pages, a natural next step would be to become acquainted with sevenths (7th). A seventh is a common note added beyond the standard three note chord. There are two main types of sevenths. One is the Major seventh and is used to add a "jazzy" sound. The second is a minor seventh and is common in many pop and rock songs.

Major 7ths

A Major 7th chord is created by adding the seventh note of the scale to the first chord that can be made in that scale. For example, a C Major seventh chord is created using a C scale and adding the seventh note, B, to the C Major chord. See Figures 1 and 2 below for examples of the C Major 7th (CMaj7) and G Major 7th (GMaj7) chords.

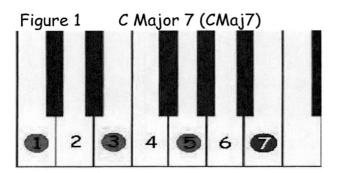

Figure 1   C Major 7 (CMaj7)

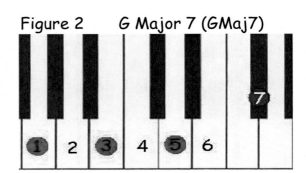

Figure 2   G Major 7 (GMaj7)

Minor 7ths

There are two main types of minor 7th chords. One, the Dominant 7th, is created using a Major chord with a minor 7th. The other is made using a minor chord and adding a minor 7th.

Dominant 7ths

The term dominant refers to the chord that occurs on the 5th note of a scale. So in the key of C, the Dominant chord would be built off the note G. It is called a dominant chord because this chord creates a sound that leads the listener's ear back to the name of the scale, in this case is C. Just as the Major 7th chord is built off of the first note of a scale, the Dominant 7th chord is built off the fifth note of a scale. So in the key of C, the Dominant 7th chord would be built off the note G. As with Major 7ths, count up 7 scale notes starting with G as 1. The resulting note would be F. A Dominant 7th chord would have the chord G (G-B-D) as its base with the 7th, F, added. See Figures 3 and 4 below for examples of the G Dominant 7th (G7) and C Dominant 7th (C7) chords.

Figure 3   G Dominant 7 (G7)

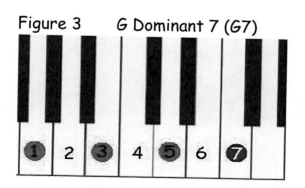

Figure 4   C Dominant 7 (C7)

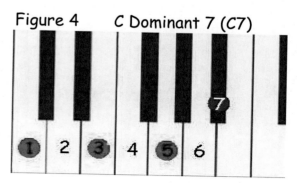

In Figure 4, C is the Dominant of the key of F. The Bb is from the key of F.

Minor Chord, Minor 7th

A minor 7th chord which is built off a minor chord can be created in a similar fashion as previously mentioned. Using the key of C as an example, D minor can be made into a minor 7th chord by adding the note that is 7 notes above D in the C scale starting with D as 1. The resulting note is C. So, a D minor 7th chord (Dm7) is made up of the notes D-F-A-C. See Figures 5 and 6 below for examples of the D minor 7th (Dm7) and B minor 7th (Bm7) chords.

Figure 5   D minor 7 (Dm7)

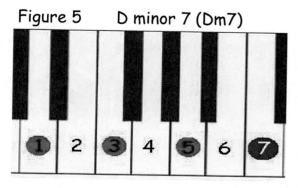

Figure 6   B minor 7 (Bm7)

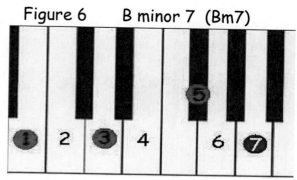

Just as three note chords can be played in inversions, so too can four note chords such as the 7ths just discussed. The same techniques for creating inversions applies for four note chords.

The methods discussed here are not the only way to create or understand Major and minor 7th chords. However, based on the information presented in this book, it is a concise and natural way to progress the reader's understanding of how chords are created and used.

Using Roman Numerals to Transpose

The chords in this book are displayed in a number of ways. One of the ways in which they are shown is through their Roman numeral with relation to their key. The way the numeral system works is each chord is given a number which corresponds to its position in relation to the scale that it is in. So a Roman numeral I (one) chord is a chord made from the first note in a scale. It is spelled with an uppercase numeral because it is a major chord. A ii (two) chord is built off of the second scale degree. It is written in lowercase numerals because it is a minor chord. In the key of C, the chords and their corresponding numerals are as follows:

C	dm	em	F	G	am	bdim
I	ii	iii	IV	V	vi	vii°

Each chord within a scale has a different function. As discussed on the previous page, the Dominant or V (five) chord has a sound that leads to the I chord. The ii chord has a sound that leads nicely to the V chord. In most pop songs, chord progressions are built off of these leading functions which is what makes them sound natural and pleasing to the ear.

One benefit of knowing and using the Roman numeral system is that it allows a performer to transpose (move) a song from its original key to another key without much thought. The method to do this is as follows: Look first at what key the song is in and figure out what the Roman numerals are for each chord. Then choose a different key and play the chords that correspond to those Roman numerals. The result will be the same song in a new key.

For example, let's look at a song that is written in the key of C and has the following chord progression: C—Am—F—G. The first thing we want to do is figure out the Roman numerals for those chords. The corresponding Roman numerals would be C = I, Am = vi, F = IV, and G = V. Now, we can go to any key we choose and apply those Roman numerals to that key to play the song. Let's choose the key of Ab. Roman numeral I in the key of Ab is the chord Ab major. Roman numeral vi in the key of Ab is the chord F minor. IV is Db major and V is Eb major. Now, if we were to play the progression Ab—Fm—Db—Eb it would be equivalent to the first progression, just in the new key of Ab. This can be very useful to know when working with singers and other musicians.

Common Chord Progressions

Below are a series of common chord progressions. They are displayed in the key of C but can be transposed to any key using the method on the opposite page. Typically each chord would be given a four count.

12 bar blues progression
C7-C7-C7-C7-F7-F7-C7-C7-G7-F7-C7-C7

Common turnaround
C-Am-Dm-G7

Common jazz progression (Circle of 5ths)
Am-Dm-G-C-F-Bdim-E

Common rock progression
C-F-G-F

Rock-n-roll progression popular in the 50's and 60's
C-Am-F-G

Common variation of previous progression
C-Am-G-F

Nice progressions with many uses
Am-F-C-G

C-G-Am-F

C-G/B-Am-C/G-F-G

C-F-C-G

For video lessons and other useful information or to order additional books, please visit

www.ThePianoChordBook.com

Made in the USA
Middletown, DE
24 February 2015